Visibility is Power

Discover the Power
of Being Seen and Heard

Roshanda E. Pratt

Please direct all copyright inquiries to:
showup@theroshowlive.com

eBook ISBN: 978-1-7356546-8-3
Paperback ISBN: 978-1-7356546-9-0

Cover and Interior Design: B.O.Y. Enterprises, Inc.
Author Photo: Aaron Smalls

Printed in the United States.

Dedication

This book is dedicated to my maternal grandmother affectionately called Mother and paternal grandmother known as Danaan. Both of these women have impacted my life in various ways. Mother taught me books before boys and Danaan sparked a love of storytelling from her animated stories of life in Trinidad and Tobago.

These women, although they may not be known in the history books, could very well be considered a hidden figure until now. I am reminded often they are part of those cloud of witnesses scripture speaks of. They believed but never saw it happen until now.

May my words reveal the essence of their strength and beauty.

I am Danaan and Mother's wildest dreams.

VISIBILITY IS POWER
Foreword by Dr. Cheryl Wood

 There is a potent expression I get to share with the women that I support globally on their personal and professional journey of growth. And that expression is, "Visibility trumps Ability." The harsh reality in life, the workplace and the marketplace today is that your talent and gifts alone will never magically usher you into your greatness. Instead, intentionally becoming visible in order to gain access to the opportunities that align you with your destiny is what will produce the greatest results. You don't get what you deserve, you only get what you demand. Remaining visible is a strong indicator you are demanding the world to see and acknowledge your greatness. Your *ability* will certainly be a major contributing factor to reaching your fullest potential and, ultimately, dictate your credibility and longevity; however, *visibility* is what will land your foot in the doors that produce the opportunities to constantly demonstrate your ability. That means, *Visibility Is Power*!

So, the question remains, why don't more people show up and make themselves visible in order to achieve what they want? Why do so many people sit on their gifts and stay quietly tucked in the background while feeling completely invisible in the world? *Visibility Is Power* provides the pivotal answer…

"Part of playing your hand and betting on you is understanding the strength of what is already inside of you. You have the goods and what you don't possess right now, you can cultivate. You are not empty and none of your experiences are wasted."

Too many of us do not acknowledge the power of what is already inside of us. Instead, we diminish and devalue who we are, what we know, what we have experienced, and what we are capable of achieving. In order to boldly come from out of the shadows and step into a life of visibility, you must acknowledge that you are enough, you are worthy, and you are capable just as you are. You must take ownership of your own destiny and realize that no one owes you anything, so you must stand up for yourself. You must courageously face your fears about feeling inadequate, your fears about being judged, and your fears about potential failure. And you must unleash your hidden greatness by coming to the forefront to speak your truth, pursue your dreams, impact the lives of others, and create an unforgettable legacy.

That is what I admire most about the author of *Visibility Is Power*, Roshanda Pratt. She has become a force to be reckoned with, not because it was easy or because anyone gave her permission to be visible, but because she made the decision to be visible. She refused to press mute on her voice or to sit on her God-given gifts because she knew the world was waiting on her. I have had the joy of connecting and engaging with Roshanda in a number of in-person settings, and I am always inspired by how powerfully and authentically she shows up in every space. And, after she shows up, she speaks up to let you know that her voice is valuable in the room. That is the result of years of self-work – eliminating the need for validation from others, becoming more self-aware and self-assured, and consistently reaffirming her own power. As stated so eloquently by Roshanda in *Visibility Is Power*, "In order for your visibility to be powerful, you have to get over what others may think about you. You cannot embrace fully your assignment, if you are willing to assign others' limited beliefs to your life." Roshanda walks the talk and demonstrates firsthand the power of visibility. She emphatically impresses upon her clients the ongoing need to eliminate toxic words, thoughts, behaviors, and people from their lives so they too can become visible, powerful, and impactful!

You are in for a soul-stirring experience by reading *Visibility Is Power*. After carefully combing through the robust pages of strategies, insights, and real-life stories, you will feel more inspired than ever before to intentionally increase your visibility and pursue your life's purpose with greater tenacity. This beautifully written piece of work by Roshanda Pratt is intriguing, inspiring, and an integral reminder that we all have the ability to take our lives to the next level and to avail ourselves of unlimited possibilities when we become bold enough to be visible.

Visibility Is Power will be a blessing to your life. It will serve as a powerful and profound reminder that nothing can hold you back from achieving greatness except your own limited beliefs. I am confident that after reading this book, you will develop an increased sense of urgency about increasing your visibility and showing up power-fully, purposefully, and passionately!

Dr. Cheryl Wood
International Motivational Speaker
& Master Speaker Development Coach

www.CherylEmpowers.com
IG/FB: @CherylEmpowers

TABLE OF CONTENTS

The Truth About Visibility

To the Jews who had believed him, Jesus said, "If you hold to my teaching, you are really my disciples. 32Then you will know the truth, and the truth will set you free."
John 8:31-32 NIV

The truth is you cannot stay the same. Think about that, right where you are, you can't stay the same. Regardless of whether you are successful and rich, or not-so-successful and far from wealthy, staying the same and doing the same things has gotten you the same results. To see what you've never seen before, you need a mindset change. Two things you can do for yourself are, 1) make a decision and 2) decide to change your mind. I need you to decide to change your mind.

There is a mind shift that is required to truly embrace your visibility. Sure, this chapter could have very well been at the end of the book. However, in order to see any true changes in your life, you must first change your mindset. We often treat mindset as an afterthought. In fact, I use to scoff at people who took on the subject of mindset, and yet here we are. I honestly said to myself, is shifting my mindset really that serious? As a person continually striving to become the better version of myself, let me tell you it is important. One of the most ancient books talks about renewing the mind. Romans 12:2 NIV states,

Visibility is Power

"Do not conform to the pattern of this world, but be transformed by the renewing of your mind. Then you will be able to test and approve what God's will is--his good, pleasing and perfect will."

There is a pattern of small thinking in our world. Therefore, there is also a pattern of small doing. You have to decide to become the pattern breaker. As a man thinks, so he becomes.

Since launching this mantra, assignment, and conviction of **Visibility is Power**, I've met people all across the country who struggle with becoming ALL God created them to be. In some cases, it is the struggle between who they are now and what they know they can be. Some shrink back because they have become accustomed to being the underdog. For others, the struggle is a spiritual one. The struggle between being humble and what may appear as prideful. But I do not believe it is prideful to show up and live fully as God created you. I believe it is an indictment towards God. There does not have be a choice between one or the other. You can be fully in your assignment, and honor it by way of recognition as you serve others. In fact, you can humbly serve others through your gift.

Jesus said, if you want to be great, you must serve. Serving people in your purpose or gift is service. Every stage, every live video, every media appearance, and every book is me taking my life experiences, journey, and purpose to serve people. To not show up fully in all areas God has created you to impact humanity, leaves a hole in our society. For every problem currently present, God has presented a solution through the witty inventions released in and by man. By nature, we are solvers. Adam solved the first problem when he named the animals. He was able to do this by showing up fully in his assignment. The moment Adam relinquished his authority, sin entered the Earth. By giving his visibility to someone else, Adam essentially forfeited his authority.

To avoid making the same mistake Adam made, you must recognize, accept, and embrace the fact that you are the solution. You were created to solve problems. Everything you use from the toothbrush to your smartphone comes from people who embraced the fact that they are the solution the world needs. Dozens of scientists, programmers and engineers told us we needed the internet. The internet has completely transformed the way we communicate. Global positioning systems (GPS) originated for the US military but the technology eventually rolled out to civilians. The development of the internet and mobile broad brand made it easier to navigate new places. And who knew we needed flat screen televisions? I remember growing up with clunky television, but digital imagining changed the way we scale images, allowing for sharp, quality visuals regardless of your screen size. I think you would agree these things made history because bold individuals embraced that they are not only the solution, but took action on their desire to create a new narrative.

For two years, I have spoken at Cervivor School, an event for cervical cancer patients and survivors. The second year, when I returned to teach on advocacy through storytelling, three ladies from the previous year were not in attendance. They had lost their battle with cancer. This retreat is always one I look forward to. While the participants always have kind remarks about how impactful the teaching is, I receive far more from the group. Life becomes real when it becomes a matter of life and death.

And because I do not know the certainty of who will return the next year, I make a point to challenge them to show up boldly because their life and others depend on it.

This particular year, towards the end of my presentation I shared the stories of people who changed history by showing up and turning their pain into purpose. I want to share two of those stories with you. 14 year-old Emmett Till was abducted at gunpoint accused of having whistled at a white woman in a grocery store. His body was found days later. Till had been brutally beaten and shot in the head. His mother decided to have an open casket to show the word the brutality of racism. Till became the face of the civil rights movement. No longer could people deny what was happening in the South. Candy Lightner's 13 year-old daughter was killed by a repeat DWI offender. She founded MADD- Mothers Against Drunk Driving. Before MADD, there were little to no legal consequences for driving while intoxicated. The truth is, in both these instances it would be easy for both Emmett Till's Family and Candy Lightner to take what happened and do nothing. But the truth is, not doing anything has not worked.

Doing nothing didn't reveal the evil of racism. It was the bold action of Emmett Till's mother allowing the world to see the swollen and bloody body of her son that gave the world undeniable proof hatred still walked among them. Prior to Candy Lightner, those driving while intoxicated never faced real lawful consequences for their decisions. In accepting the power of her visibility, she used her voice to cause change in legislation all over the country. In both these instances, there had to be a mindset embraced that I can no longer stand by and not do anything to change this! There had to be a mindset that went beyond their personal pain to purpose.

The first year at Cervivor School, I met a woman who shared her story. She grew up poor, a victim of sexual assault and now cervical cancer. In her words, it was another thing happening to her. Without hesitation, I walked over to her and pointed my finger and said, "You make cancer pay. Make cancer feel sorry for ever missing with you!" What was I doing? I was helping her to shift the mindset. It is not happening to you but happening *for you*, so that you can become the instigator that changes it for others. Every movement, every person we read about in history, came up against an obstacle they could hide in or show up, look "it" in the face and handle it.

One year later, when I returned to Cervivor School I almost did not recognize her. She looked empowered and told me she spent the year making cancer pay! She started speaking more, sharing her story. Making Cancer Pay became her mantra and she even pushed for the group to turn the phrase into a t-shirt. WOW! A complete mind shift around her circumstances changed how she showed up. Listen, I don't know what your "IT" is. What the thing is that can be a thorn in your side, a pain in your heart, or a tragedy so horrific you can't see anything good coming from it, but I am here to say you are no longer allowed to stay the same. It is time for you to embrace your authority and begin to change the narrative!

Surviving sexual assault on numerous occasions is what drove me to become a storyteller. Years of being hushed into silence, told not to say anything and believing the lie of my voice didn't matter put me in a space of self-discovery. When I found my voice, I knew I wanted to empower others to do the same. When my mind shifted from focusing on the pain itself, to embracing the purpose attached to the pain, it became a total game changer. Showing up was no longer an option. It was a necessity. It was necessary for the people I am called to serve, my legacy, and the world looking for an answer.

Likewise, your visibility can no longer be an option. You have an assignment to help change the narrative. You can't do that if you never show up. There is a state of emergency and you are the 9-1-1 first responder. We need you on assignment. You aren't called to visibility because God ran out of tasks for you to do. You are called to visibility because we need you. Romans 8:19 reads, For the creation waits in eager expectation for the children of God to be revealed. SHOW YOURSELF! The truth about visibility is you have to set yourself free from your own limitations and boundaries. Be honest with yourself, have your own limitations and boundaries served you well thus far? Embrace the truth of your story, but ask yourself, how can I start to rewrite this?

I am amazed at the people I get to work with to help them uncover their story, understand their mission, and make profit from it. In many instances, once I start to dig deeper, I discover I am speaking to a survivor of sexual assault or someone who has been violated in some way. I do not believe that is a coincidence. I believe it's an opportunity for me to empower them to walk the journey of their truth and re-write their story. Remember, as a man thinks, so he is. Changing the narrative begins with changing your internal perspective. It is time to see our truth as an opportunity of purpose and not a place of pain. The journey starts now. You have to be willing to let go of your stinking thinking. You have to be open to looking at the thing that hurt you from another perspective. I want you to be open to being challenged and allow God to speak to your heart about what needs to change. Because the truth is, you cannot stay the same. Staying the same is too dangerous and your purpose is too valuable.

Over the next few chapters, we are going to explore my path to realizing visibility is power. We'll discuss the painful moments I later learned were actually opportunities to discover the power of my own narrative, the transformative lessons learned, and questions for you to explore at the end of each chapter. You will also read the stories of other men and women who discovered their visibility and the impact it has had on their life. My hope and prayer is for our stories give you hope, grace, and power to move from the shadows of your life. It is time for you to shine.

V.I.P. QUESTIONS

What limited mindset do you need to let go of in order to be seen?

_____

_____

_____

_____

_____

_____

_____

_____

_____

How can you move past those limited beliefs?

_____

_____

_____

_____

_____

_____

_____

_____

_____

Play Your Hand
My Visibility Story

"I decided to bet on me because I can't lose, I know what I am capable of doing." -Roshanda E. Pratt

"Thank you for applying, but we cannot hire you as a reporter at this time."

That's essentially what my first rejection letter stated. I had applied for a position as a television news reporter. I was rejected. I was not wanted. I still have that letter today. Seriously, if I think about it, I was not ready. I did not like my voice. I did not like how I looked on camera. I lacked confidence. I was afraid. I had a grocery list of "no's." Can you relate? It is one thing to have others reject you, but it is a different kind of sting to reject yourself, to count yourself out. I felt my life was a series of *The Little Engine That Could* mantra's... I think I can, I think I can. Believing in me became one of the most powerful revelations next to discovering God's love for me.

I started working in television news while I was still a stu-

dent at Winthrop University. I knew what I wanted from the time I set foot on campus. I wanted to be an anchor woman. My love for television news started in the fourth grade when my West Indian father would make me watch the news. He told me it was my responsibility to know what is going on in my country and community. I was hooked. I looked forward to catching the evening news with either Walter Cronkite, Peter Jennings or Tom Brokaw. In that time, there were not many women on the main anchor desk. But I knew I would impact the industry in some way. I prepared for my future. While in college, I purchased what I call the anchor suit. These are nicely fit-ted in the waist suits in various colors from then Casual Corner. I let my hair grow out to a bob length with just enough highlights. My muse: Barbara Walters, mixed with a little Connie Chung topped with Oprah. Back in those days on Winthrop University's campus, I was known as the "next" Oprah. I had it figured out, at least that is what I thought. I would work in the local news market for a while until Oprah decided she was done with her talk show. That is when she would exit stage left and insert me as the new boss.

My plan never happened. I think sometimes God may look at our plans and laugh. When you think about it, it is rather silly. When has the clay ever told the potter what it wanted to become? NEVER. My first paying television position, I "slid" into it as a news assistant. In television, you take the job that's given and hope to climb the ladder to your next position. Within six months or so, I was promoted to Associate Producer and was on the fast track to becoming a full-time producer. I learned how to write and work with reporters and producers. I discovered the art of pitching stories, how to put a show together, and the art of multi-tasking. Every once in a while, I even had the opportunity to work outside the newsroom, field producing content for air. Those years I had the privilege of covering the biggest stories in our nation's history, 9-11, the war on terror, Former Carolina Panther, Rae Carruth trial, and Hurricanes just to name a few of the headlines.

It was exhilarating to be on the frontlines, for an up-close look at history from the television news producer chair. Yet, I still desired to truly be on the frontlines, out in the field as a reporter and ultimately landing on the anchor desk.

College allowed me to put together a reel showing my "reporter" skills. I flubbed. It was painful. I couldn't get it out of my head. I hated it. Until this point, I felt I was a confident person, but that diminished. I realized my dreams of wanting to be on camera may never happen because I was fearful and lacked confidence. I compared myself to other reporters. It crippled me. I compared my beginning story to their middle. There had always been a little engine that could inside of me, an internal motivation that kept me going in the face of adversity. Each time I compared myself to another report, lost her steam.

Friends, comparison really is a thief. We compare ourselves to others without knowing the scope of their story. What a lie! Just imagine, as a producer I am writing the words news anchors or reporters would read on air. Yet, I could not read those very same words. They were mine, but honestly, I did not own them like they first belonged to me. They were my intellectual property. But I gave my words away as part of the job and did not see the value in what I brought to the table. There was a constant internal war. My struggle was exacerbated by the fact that God assured me I was to be in the forefront of media, not the background. I spent the greater part of my professional journalism career writing, creating, assisting and shaping news content from the producer's chair, behind the scenes.

In 2015, while I was the Executive morning show producer for a local CBS affiliate, a shift happened. Our morning team had just finished a 2.5-hour morning show. CBS This Morning came on and like any other morning, we started watching. A tech segment came on to discuss two new apps: Meerkat and Periscope. Both helped average Joes turn their smartphones into media networks of sorts. Through these apps you could go live anywhere. Eureka! I was elated. I stayed glued to that television screen. I felt like I just hit gold. I told my colleagues, "Do you guys see this?" They were not excited.

One of the first steps to visibility, if I had to put it in steps, know when to shift, pivot and embrace something new. Periscope quickly dwarfed its predecessor, Meerkat, and became very popular among live-streaming apps. Within the first 30 days, thousands downloaded the app, but many did not know what to do with it nor how it worked. But we who immediately jumped on it, knew in some way this could be the fire to light our visibility. I began testing it out.

Although a bit clumsy, I started treating it not as a status update, but a television broadcast. People started watching, even colleagues at the station. I had a few naysayers, who did not get the concept. They would often ask; what does she think she is doing? Some mocked and joked. I imagine this is the same way they probably laughed at and mocked Albert Einstein, Oprah and Noah who built an ark while it wasn't raining.

In order for your visibility to be powerful, you have to get over what others may think about you. You cannot fully embrace your assignment, if you are willing to assign others limited beliefs to your life. All the permission you need comes from God. You don't have to ask for permission when it has already been granted by God.

When I embraced this truth and my voice, *The Rosho Live* started to take shape and became a "thing." I started going live from the newsroom with one of my colleagues. I went live every chance I could get, even after working a third shift. I was determined this was MY MOMENT. My mentor and friend, Tia Brewer-Footman says, "Momentum waits for no one and it doesn't require giving you and encore." I knew this was the moment, I saw many years prior.

When I lived in rural South Carolina, staring out the back window at my overgrown grass, serving in ministry, new mom and no longer in television, I knew then I was already, The Rosho Live. The rest of the world just hadn't seen it yet. God told me then how my future was to look, but nothing in the present communicated that. Back then, there was no live video. I had my television experience,

16

but I left to pursue a "higher" calling. I know this for sure, if people engage with me, they will want to do business with me. I knew this was the way to get people to engage with me. I felt, to know me is to love me. Some might say that is arrogant, nope it's understanding your secret sauce. But there was still this lingering issue. I did not like how I looked or sounded on camera. I was my worst critic. I did not have a hater; I was my hater.

So, with very little money as I was a budding entrepreneur, I took a video creation course. Many of the things I knew, but what I learned from that course is, I could not treat video like we did broadcast news. I had to be willing to be vulnerable and transparent. I committed to sharing the real me; the quirky, bold, sometimes loud, and plain truth talking me.

I started with the personality I felt people would buy. I had to be willing to show up! So, scared as scared could be, I hit the record button on my laptop and started recording videos to upload to YouTube. I keep those videos with very little energy and mostly scripted, as a reminder of how far I've evolved in meeting the real me. There is a real you, you have not met yet. While I enjoyed recorded video, it still felt canned, but when live video came, it felt like an energy overload.

I loved the instant feedback in the comments whether they were good or bad, (I had a few). I loved seeing the flurry of hearts filling the screen because people loved what I was sharing. I love the community and relation-ships built. Live video gave me a community. Live video really is a game changer. I became known in the digital streets as the storyteller, live video strategist, and heart-felt producer.

In 2017, I wrote a book titled *CEO Of Live Video* teaching people how to connect and convert their live audience. While in my third trimester of pregnancy, I birthed this book to equip any messenger to go live on purpose, for a purpose. In 24 hours, it became an Amazon Bestseller and won in the social media category. How did it happen? I wasn't thinking about writing a book at that time. But, The LinkedIn Professor, Tijuana Ross, challenged me and I am always up for a good challenge. Essentially, she was chal-lenging me to show up to own my visibility. She told me a book helps you to own your genius and expertise. It is true. You have an area of expertise. OWN IT. For far too long, we have been hidden figures instead of pioneers of unfamiliar territory.

Amelia Earhart is an American aviation pioneer. Earhart was the first female aviator to fly solo across the Atlantic Ocean. She set many records and wrote best-selling books. During an attempt to make a circumnavigational flight of the globe in 1937, Earhart and her navigator dis-appeared over the central Pacific Ocean. Some might say

Earhart failed, but I looked at her life with much fascination. She was willing to do what others did not. In a time when aviation was still taking off, (no pun intended), Earhart launched into uncharted territory to pave a pathway for others to do the same. When you own your visibility, it empowers others to own theirs. This is why your visibility is power. Your visibility is not about you.

As a young child, I remember playing the game follow the leader. Our world is still looking to follow the leader. Visibility is leadership, taking the lead and lighting the way for others to do the same. As a storyteller and live stream strategist, I know my call is to raise up a group of fearless messengers. The world is waiting for you to step out of the shadows into the light. I think of the song we teach kids in Sunday school.

> This little light of mine,
> I'm gonna let it shine.
> This little light of mine,
> I'm gonna let it shine.
> This little light of mine,
> Yes, I'm gonna let it shine.
> Let it shine, let it shine, let it shine.

I get what the song is saying, but why a little light? It's the little light I often see as a problem for my clients. They are so stuck on being little they have a hard time embracing GOING BIG or living BIGGER. I say this

BIG light of mine, I'm going to let it shine. People are attracted to the light. It is the light that draws.

In order to let your big light shine, you have to decide to bet on yourself, you have to decide that you have all the cards in your hand to win. Yes, you have the goods for your ideal audience or client. You have the goods to serve them well. You have the goods God gave you to show up. YOU NEED TO BET ON YOU! Is it risky? Yes. But you are worth the risk.

I remember when I left my job as a multi-platform producer at the news station for full-time entrepreneurship. I knew it was time to shift because I felt I could not fully embrace my visibility in that environment. I was growing a brand, *The Rosho Live*. I was a speaker with a growing Facebook Live audience, yet at work I felt like I was still in the proving stages or limited in what I really desired to do. It was a conflict I could no longer bare.

After seeking Godly counsel and talking to my husband, we decided I would leave after four years at this particular station. Something interesting happened during the following months. Opportunities were coming from every side. It felt as if people were waiting for me to leave the station to do business with me. In fact, one person confirmed that was the case. Amazing! What if there are people waiting on you?

Please understand, this is not my effort to talk you into leaving your job. I believe in entrepreneurship and employment. But I also know there are some who use their employment not as a group to cultivate their talents or as their first Angel Investor into their endeavors, but as a place to stay hidden and comfortable. For those working on a job, how are you leveraging your visibility? How are you showing up for *you* while still showing up for your employer? You have been overlooked enough. If you're honest with yourself, you'll admit you're not seen or heard.

To get the most out of this book, you must embrace the idea of being okay with being seen. Poet and Activist Nikki Giovanni, said, "You've got to find a way to make people know you're there." Do people know you are there? People are looking for solutions. Why make them work to find it? Social media has shrunk down the hunt for solutions. Live video gives us instant access to people who surf their phones looking to be entertained, educated, or empowered. The world we live in, is full of problems, but I believe those who are truly visible for the right reasons, become the solution the world is waiting on. I want you to see yourself as a solution. I want you to show up in your life everyday wondering how you can solve a problem. Don't be the problem, instead live as the problem solver. This notion helped me become accountable and stop living life solely for me and about me. Please understand you never arrive at visibility. It is a constant work in progress over a period of a lifetime. How you show up in one season is different in the next.

I need you to understand this is not just a one and done thing, but this is a conviction, an assignment and mission. This is your life. Every day, you are selling a story by your actions or inactions. Your DNA is a line of stories, a carrier of genetic information. Scientists say DNA holds the instructions for an organism or cell's development, reproduction, and ultimately death. Your DNA contains a story. You can't get away from it. Story is even woven in our scientific structure. With that being said, you cannot get away from the story of your life. Ask yourself this question. At the end of your life, do you want your story to be one of permission or denial?

My husband taught our children growing up the story of our name. He said as Pratts what we do is serve people. We are a blessing wherever we go. That is what our name means, and you can't get away from that. To do so, is to deny your make-up, who you are, your DNA. You were created to be the answer, the very embodiment of God's permission for someone else. Just as you needed to hear, see, and accept God's permission to live BIG, someone is waiting for you to reveal your story so they can follow in your footsteps.

Your story is living, and it gives life to others. Part of playing your hand and betting on you is understanding the strength of what is already inside of you. You have the goods and what you don't possess right now, you can cultivate. You are not empty and none of your experiences are wasted. My friend, whether it's a royal flush, straight flush, four of a kind or full house, you have a winning hand. Like any good poker player, focus, be patient, learn from your mistakes, adapt, but be fearless. Play your hand. Because there is more in it than you think.

I know you may feel overwhelmed by the fact that everything you need is already in you. But I want to help you process this new idea of being seen and heard. I highly encourage you to engage and answer the VIP questions as you process this new information.

V.I.P. QUESTIONS:

What is preventing your from becoming more visible?

_____

_____

_____

_____

_____

_____

What needs to happen now for you to become more visible?

_____

_____

_____

_____

_____

_____

What will you commit to in order to be seen and heard? This is an action step.

_____

_____

_____

_____

_____

_____

V.I.P. (Visibility is Power) Story:

Name: Jen Bennett

Is there a moniker you are known for, i.e., The Rosho Live Storyteller, Live Stream Strategist and Heartfelt Producer? If not, how do you want me to describe you?

#BeWorthFollowing: How to Be Different and Influence People in a Crowded Social World

What does Visibility is Power mean to you?

When I think of Visibility is Power, it reminds me of a very important marketing concept: People want to see you. People want to see the face behind a "brand." People want real, they want authenticity. And the reality is, when people see the face behind a brand, that visibility is power. Why? Because that is how you begin creating a community, a tribe of people that will come to trust you and be your biggest cheerleaders.

Briefly share your Visibility story:

If I'm honest, I've always been a words kinda gal. I enjoy writing words down. But in today's age of social media and videos, I've come to realize just how important videos are. I was recently chosen and invited as one of 55 social media influencers to take part in the Falcon Heavy Rocket launch in Florida. While there, I was taking lots of pictures and sharing them with my audience. But what I soon realized is that I needed to do a video, a Facebook Live video. And wouldn't you know it? All I could think about was Rosho and Visibility is Power. Needless to say, I did a few videos and my audience loved them! Were they perfect? No. But my audience, my community, enjoyed seeing the experience from my perspective. They enjoyed getting a behind the scenes look at my experience at NASA. And what I love is that after my live videos, they shared with me how much they enjoyed them, again, reinforcing that Visibility is Power.

What is your favorite moment since embracing Visibility is Power?

Realizing that my audience enjoyed seeing me on video. That blew me away.

Advice for those struggling with their visibility?

Just do it! I think we can get caught up in thinking that everything has to be perfect, that the video, lighting, and words have to be absolutely perfect. But the reality is, that is not what people are looking for. They don't care about perfection, they just want to see you! So, grab your phone and go after it!

V.I.P. Tip (share your favorite Visibility tip i.e using Live Video to connect to your audience)

We are our worst critics. Again, don't feel like you have to look perfect or have the perfect hair day to do it. Just do it!

Social media handle:

@DrJenBennett on FB, IG, Twitter, LI

The Gift of Invisibility

"Invisible things are the only realities." -Edgar Allan Poe

"I feel like I am hidden, and everyone is advancing except for me!"

I will never forget those words from a young lady at an event I hosted. Her words pierced me. I knew what it felt like having a vision, a word from God and yet still find yourself in the same place. It can be crippling. It can seem like a cruel joke is being played on you. It feels like God forgot about you. But I am here to tell you friend, He hasn't and being invisible is part of the process of visibility. Invisibility is the road to becoming visible. What's hidden becomes discoverable.

This is my story of being hidden.

About 2015, before there was live video, there was static video. This is video recorded to be uploaded to then YouTube. At this time, I had left television news and started my own business, a jewelry making company called To BEad Continued. It was an amazing venture. However, I knew I belonged in front of the camera. I was terrified. Yes, I hated my voice, how I looked, and I lacked confidence. I took a video course to get over my mental roadblocks. The instructor of that online video course told us to have fun, don't treat it like news, but make video whatever I wanted it to be. Really? Make video whatever I wanted it to be? Could that be? I could create what I wanted. How liberating!

Madame C.J. Walker, one of my favorite entrepreneurs said, "I got my start by giving myself a start." I hated video, but I did it. I would record these videos about my experiences in business and life and upload them to YouTube. In fact, if you go to my YouTube page, @the-rosholive, you will see those videos. I cringe when I look at them because it is a stark contrast to where I am today. Baby, that's growth. But there is something else that happened during that time too.

It did not seem like the place or the time God could give me a platform to impact women. But it was in an obscure place that God spoke purpose. In hiding, I heard and saw the vision of The Rosho Live. God called me The Rosho Live before there was live video, an audience, a platform or anything else. Out of nothing came something rather extraordinary. Invisibility can be a gift.

In the 1960's, a television series called, *The Invisible Man* featured a British scientist named Peter Brady. He was working on an invisibility formula, when he had a tragic accident turning himself invisible. There was no antidote. While working on a method to regain his visibility, Peter undertakes missions for the government to stop the bad guys. What I find most interesting about the synopsis of the show is, Peter was "working" on the very thing that marred him being invisible. He wanted to be seen, but it was in his invisibility that he discovered himself. For Peter, in the 1960's television series, he discovered his purpose as an undercover agent for the Government. Visibility is Power, but the road to get there starts in the unknown.

As humans, we have a powerful need to be seen and heard. One of the needs of humans is the need to be accepted. We all want to feel valued, important and that we matter. But do not confuse the opportunity of being hidden as an opportunity of not being valued, highly esteemed and important. American author Ralph Ellison wrote,

> "I am an invisible man. I am a man of substance, of flesh and bone, fiber and liquids- and I might even be said to possess a mind. I am invisible, understand, simply because people refuse to see me."

Ellison said people refused to see, but sometimes the very person who refuses to see, is the person in the mirror. Before others can see you, you must first see yourself. You have to start with the man or woman in the mirror. Have you looked at yourself lately? The antidote to being invisible is embracing your season or time of hiding. In the season of hiding that is your season of discovery and building. I have learned how to embrace the seasons in my life of not being noticed.

One of my business coaches told me, "Roshanda build deep and in silence." She used the analogy of the Titanic. The ocean liner struck an iceberg during its maiden voyage. My coach told me how the passengers saw the top of the iceberg but did not see how deep the ice was beneath the water. In this season of being hidden, build deep. Build structure in your business and personal life. Build deep relationships, as relationships are currency. Your network determines your net worth. Over the years, as I've examined my life, there were times when I didn't have stacks of money in my bank account. However, I was rich in relationships, rich in people who would recommend me for opportunities, rich in people who shared the impact I made on their life with others, rich in the amount of influence my life and message have had on others as well as people who used their influence to refer me for opportunities that resulted in increased income. You can make impact, influence, and income through the richness of your relationships, the same way you can with your visibility. This is why relationships are valuable currency that you must spend wisely.

Make time to review your relationships and build a team while you are in hiding because no one can do anything significant without support. Build systems and strategies that set you up for success. In hiding is the best time to build because when visibility shows up, it is time to **SHOW UP**! You won't have time to build when you are busy showing up! Those times in hiding are not wasted, they are the perfect moments to build deep!

Your character, business acumen and knowledge are built in times of hiding. Do not despise it, embrace it. There is power in silence. Speakers use the power of silence or pause for emphasis or to get their audience to think. This season of hiding you are in, is your time to think. It is the time to put emphasis on the things which will cause you to be prepared for the next season of unveiling. I often tell clients when it comes to sharing your story, share what you are comfortable and healed from. Tell your story from a place of victory. There is no greater discomfort than sitting in an audience on live video and watching people tell their story from a broken or unresolved place. It is hard to watch someone attempt to deal with complexities and emotions of their story in front of people.

Allow what needs to take place during your wait. We live in a world that measures success by how much you are seen. The conviction of Visibility is Power is that you are seen and heard; however, the greater thrust is that you are using your visibility to make profound impact. We step out of hiding to step into being visible in order to give others permission to do the same. Please do not get wrapped up in a culture and rush your process. Just imagine the baby chick that rushes its birth process.

I remember in elementary school, we did a science project on the hatching of baby chicks. We had an incubator set up in a cage creating this atmosphere to facilitate the hatching. Environment is critical. The heat source of the incubator, the right measure of humidity is necessary for the chickens to hatch without problem. Everything is contingent upon the right environment for something that is hidden. Did you catch that? When our class maintained the right environment, it was only a matter of time before the chicken hatched. How does this apply to you? When I maintain the necessary environment what was once invisible, will soon be revealed. Don't rush the process. This is your time of incubation. Every step of the incubation process is important for you to achieve the end result you desire.

Every step, every day makes a difference. Invisibility is the process to visibility. Media Mogul, Oprah Winfrey speaking to the graduating class of 2019 at Colorado College shared success is a process not just some big break. "It's actually about taking one significant life-transforming step at a time," she explained. "Small steps lead to big accomplishments."

In other words, every action every day builds upon those from the previous day. The old adage is correct, slow and steady wins the race or in this case, leads to success. The 20 years I spent behind the scenes as a television news producer taught me invaluable lessons about media production. It prepared me for a moment in 2018, when the local CBS affiliate I was working for had breaking news of a major interstate shut down as a man held himself hostage.

The news director at the time drew me and a few people into the coverage live on television. My job was to provide people alternate routes around this interstate. After our noon show, the news director asked me to go live on Facebook for an undetermined length of time discussing the breaking news. I later learned from one of my colleagues she was concerned if I could do it. They responded with have you seen her on Facebook live? She can do it and I did. Not perfectly, but I did it.

Honestly, your audience doesn't want perfection just progress wrapped in accurate information. How was I able to do it? The years I spent behind the scenes watching reporters live in the field. The times I would see my anchors and network anchors adlib breaking news. I studied them and even practiced at home in front of my mirror. Success is planned. I practiced in obscurity for my moment in visibility. So, that morning when I was headed to work like every morning, I dressed like that day was the day I would be on air, because I knew I was supposed to be in front of the camera. I knew despite what was presently in front of me, my time would come even if my circumstances did not show it yet. You see time and chance happen to us all. (Eccl. 9:11 NIV)

While you are hidden, you **MUST** be convinced of where you know you are supposed to be. You must be convinced more than anyone else even while your circumstances do not look like it. I came into the television business to be a reporter/anchor. But I took the path of a producer because that was the job available, it was what was needed and it's the path others decided for me. I have no regrets. Although I hid behind the scenes, it was behind the scenes where I learned. This moment in hiding is your training ground. I surprised myself and a few others in that newsroom. Do not despise these small beginnings because they are leading to bigger steps of success.

In the moments when you doubt, remind yourself of what is true. I know it is easier said than done, but I would tell myself, I am right where I am supposed to be. I am not behind in my purpose, but right on schedule. Those statements were my affirmations, or simply put, truth statements that affirmed me and shifted my perspective. What TRUTH are you telling yourself? I want to give you an opportunity right now to take a few moments to write those things down.

This is a reminder when you question yourself, that the following is what's really true:

_____
_____
_____
_____
_____
_____
_____
_____
_____

Although, you are in a hiding place for preparation, the key word is preparation. You are not in hiding just for the sake of hiding. Have an honest conversation with yourself. You know when you are not playing fully. Do not use this time to overthink or find an excuse to shrink back. Ask yourself the hard questions and dig deep to discover why you are hiding.

This season of hiding can happen more than once in different ways. I remember two seasons in particular, God had me in hiding to protect the gift and call He has on my life and needed to align me with the right relationships to help draw that out. But there was also a time I put myself in hiding because of overwhelming fear of messing up. Where are you? It is important to know. Even if the time of hiding is self-imposed, why is it? I know I had a friend who had a season of being still and quiet because she was working on being humble. You have to know where you are in order to discover where you are going.

I am in hiding for:

_____

_____

_____

_____

_____

_____

_____

_____

_____

_____

_____

_____

_____

Famed poet, Maya Angelou says, *"We delight in the beauty of the butterfly, but rarely admit the changes it has gone through to achieve that beauty."* Before the butterfly can ever spread its wings, it has a four-stage insect life cycle it must go through. Let's head back to science class briefly, you have the egg, larva, pupa and adult.

Each stage has a different goal, and the life cycle process can take a month to a year depending on the type of butterfly. The butterfly will lay eggs on a leaf, about five days later a tiny worm-like creature will hatch from the egg. In the second stage of being a caterpillar, sometimes called larvae it starts to eat leaves and flowers. It eats all the time. It eats the leaf that it was born on. This is the eating and growing stage. It grows so fast; it becomes too big for its skin. So, the creepy crawly caterpillar has to shed its old skin. It grows new skin and sheds it four or more times while growing. In this stage, they're known as chrysalis or pupa.

In this stage of protection, the caterpillar is mostly brown or green, the same color as the things around it. This is so other animals will not see it. Did you catch that? Even the beautiful butterfly has had a season of being invisible, hidden for its own protection. Experts say this is the resting stage and the changing stage. The caterpillar starts to change into a butterfly. It looks different, its shape starts to change, all of this happens in chrysalis. When metamorphosis is complete, the pupal skin splits and the insect climbs out. Now you would think it is ready to fly, but that is not the case. The butterfly's wings are folded against its body. The butterfly is also very tired, so it rests. Once it has rested, it will be ready to start flying. They can't fly well at first but are quick learners. They will look for food, soon find a mate, lay eggs and start the life cycle all over again.

I took the time to go through the lengthy process of a butterfly because much our life can mirror the life cycle of a butterfly. From the seed of an idea, spending time with that idea, growing that idea and then releasing it to the world. You are experiencing your own metamorphosis. While it may be uncomfortable and a tad bit ugly, the fruit that comes from it is a beautiful journey. I cannot begin to tell you how many messages I have received over the years once I understood my metamorphosis is not just about me nor for me. My journey getting here was shrouded in low self-esteem, sexual trauma, failure, depression and self-sabotage. I used my issues as reasons why it could never happen for me instead of understanding my mess helped to create the message that would impact the world. The mess... my cocoon is what helped shape me into the beautiful butterfly I am today. It has been said, "Butterflies can't see their wings. They can't see how truly beautiful they are but everyone else can."

What a freedom experienced when I started embracing all of my story. I gained my wings and I could soar. But this moment could have never happened without my time in isolation. Every messenger, influencer, thought leader and game changer goes through their time wrapped in a cocoon preparing for their release to the world. The caterpillar is never stressed or worried about how long they are in "hiding" they just know this is part of the process. Process. We love the outcome but hate the process. My fitness trainer tells us all the time the process outweighs the end goal. As I heard one woman say, marry the process and divorce the outcome. Wow. Invisibility is part of the process of showing up. Environmentally, butterflies help flowers pollinate, eat weedy plants and provide a food source for other animals. The presence or absence can tell us a lot about the local environment. Just like the butterfly, you have an important purpose to the function of this world. You are a source of hope and inspiration for others. Your presence, or the lack of it, can affect all of us. This is why you no longer can be comfortable being in the cocoon phase for too long. Your visibility is power, and it can bring profit.

Enjoy your transformation into Visibility, Impact, and Profit. Because once you finally break forth, there is no going back. When you finally get wind under your wings, there is no slowing down.

Visibility is Power

Significant Visibility

"I won't let you die, I have something significant for you to do."

-God

When I was 7 or 8 years old, I remember it was a stormy night in Saginaw, Michigan. Besides being a stormy night, I remember feeling this heavy presence of death in my room. I was not at peace and even at that young age I knew something was wrong. Trauma taught me how to know sense danger. I could not explain it but I knew it was an experience that was not safe. I walked to my teenage sister's room. She was ten years older than me. She couldn't offer anything but to tell me to go pray. In our family and upbringing there was not a spiritual foundation beyond superstition and traditional West Indian practices. Our prayers involved the popular, Now I lay me down to sleep. If you are not familiar it goes as follows:

> Now I lay me down to sleep.
> I pray the Lord my soul to keep.
> If I should die before I wake,
> I pray to God my soul to take.
> If I should live for other days...

Honestly, it is the creepiest prayer we can teach children to recite. But as I went back to bed and started to talking to God, with what very little I knew. I remember having this feeling of peace and calm fill the room. I chased for that peace for years until I gave my life to Christ. Then I heard a voice say, "You are not going to die, I have some-thing significant for you to do." For years, I have let that thought of significance chase and guide me. Even when I struggled with my own significance I knew in the back of my mind, I was created for more. You may not have had God whisper this to you. Maybe your life is like mine, starting off with very life significance but you can change the narrative. You can have a life of significance and im-pact. Noah Webster 1828 dictionary defines significance as derived from the word SIGNIFY. The word means a sign or to make. There are several definitions but there are two I want to focus on.

1. To make known something, either by signs or words; to express or communicate to another any idea, thought, wish, a nod, wink, gesture, signal or other sign.

2. To make known; to declare.

Your life is supposed to signal, a sign or declare something in the earth. You are not just here by accident. Your par-ents may not have prepared for you but God was very much aware and prepared for you to be the signal, the sign, and declaration of who He is. I think back to the moment God spoke to me as a little girl who was mo-lested, already dealing with depression and low self-esteem that my life mattered and He would in fact use it to bring Glory to His name. Years later I asked God about this "significant" work He called me to, and He told me, "eve-rything you do is significant."

WOW! I want to encourage you, your visibility is a sign of who your creator, God is. The world is still looking for a sign. Tag! You are the sign they are waiting for. Romans 8:19, states, "For the creation waits with eager longing for the revealing of the children of God." This is why it is vitally important to deal with the issue of you. Why are you comfortable being in the background when you know God is pushing you forward? Why does the voice of your pain or the negativity of what others said speak louder than what God has said about you? Why are you still waiting for a person to give you permission to do what God has already called and Graced you to do? WHY? You have to answer those questions if you want to live a life of significance. This is important because your visibility goes beyond just money, we will discuss that later, but this is eternal impact.

I was in the hair salon when a woman came up to me and grabbed my hand. She is part of my free online community on Facebook. She told me she loves watching my videos and thanked me for not giving up. She went on to say I can imagine how difficult it can be for you. I know there are things we don't see but you are showing up and giving us permission to do the same. That is significance. I want to live a life of significance. Do you?

Consider this: a butterfly, candle and city all have a certain level of significance. We can agree all three attract people in a different way. Children are memorized by the beauty of a butterfly. The candle releases a fragrance that appeals to the senses and the city sits as a beacon or representative of the prosperity of a city. Each has a different function or significance. But they all draw people to their significance. Let's focus on the candle and city. A candle lights a room, but a city illuminates blocks.

Matthew 5:15 reads, "Neither do people light a lamp and put it under a bowl. Instead they put it on its stand, and it gives light to everyone in the house." The candle or lamps lights a house. You are supposed to give light to your house, family and friends. Those closest to you should experience your light. In that same chapter verse 14 states, "You are the light of the world—like a city on a hilltop that cannot be hidden." You are a city called to bring light to the community, nation and world. This is why I have discovered visibility is power is beyond an area or zip code. It is an assignment to impact households, communities and nations. Here are two stories to demonstrate this.

The Candle

I once worked with a client by the name of Reba. She and I had a session to support her in discovering her message and the connection to those she is called to serve and impact. What we discovered was that she was missing the opportunity to work alongside her husband in a business they already had. Sometimes we are fought in the areas we could have the greatest impact. Not saying there was any fighting going on in the marriage, but we all know the challenges that can occur when working with a family member, especially a spouse.

What we discovered was that Reba needed to be visible in that relationship, and as a result of her following my recommendations, she became visible in her household. The result of owning her flame as a candle ignited her marriage, plus their business had an immediate opportunity which produced $8k and she is well on her journey of more visibility, impact and profit. It all started with embracing her influence and letting her light shine with those closest to her.

The City

People are drawn to a city. Just picturing the bright lights, the imposing structure of the buildings, and the possibilities of life in a growing metropolitan area creates an undeniable allure in most people. I experienced this growing the brand The Rosho Live. Whenever I meet Facebook friends for the first time (social media friends are real, by the way) I would hear the same narrative. You are just like you are online. You are such a bright light. This message of visibility has taken along the Southeast, Midwest and Paris, France. What people are attracted to is the bright lights and the possibilities they see in me. My light represents the same attraction as any major city's skyline on the darkest of nights. The darker the night, the brighter the lights of the city shine. When my social media friends encounter me in real life, they are drawn to the light inside of me. I am a city that can't be hidden. You are a city that can't be hidden. Turn on your light.

You don't need permission to turn on your light, permission is already granted by God. This was and continues to be a major revelation to me. There was a time, before becoming The First Lady of Visibility (insert wink), I looked for permission to do what I knew in my heart, revealed in my prayer time to do. I wanted permission from those who I deemed could give it and was disappointed when it did not happen. As humans we have this great need for approval and belonging and in some way, I wanted permission to validate what I already knew to be true. It was a major disservice to myself and those who may or may not have known this is what I was seeking. We are asking for permission when the access has already been granted by God. I am no longer doing it. I am putting down asking

43

for permission and picking up access granted. The definition of permission means; allowing or liberty granted. You have the liberty to let your light shine and the only reason it is not lighting a city is all in how you show up. The way a candle and city light a space is very different. It all goes back to capacity. A candle can light a smaller space versus a city that can illuminate blocks. Both have the same function of light just a different capacity. You must give yourself permission to show up even if it's the candle that later becomes the city. But waiting for someone to say it is okay for you to let the light of Christ to shine is not nor will it ever be okay. Visibility is Power! But that power works when you understand the power of standing in what is already available to you.

Learn to say YES to the best. Develop the habits of saying YES to bigger opportunities even if you are scared. Practice saying YES even if you don't know all the steps and just figure it out. As Marie Forleo says, "Everything is figureoutable." Understand the power of saying YES to God puts you in position for greater visibility. Let's revisit our topic of the candle and city. Where a candle is position determines how much light will be dispense and where. Where city lights are determines where it will draw people. Position matters in your visibility. Position yourself as the obvious choice and solution.

In my visibility journey when I started positioning myself as a storyteller, I saw stories everywhere. In fact, when I work with clients on creating their narrative/messaging something electrifying happens when they start talking. The words turn into pictures and I can see it all play out like a movie in front of me. When I start crafting the narrative taking into account everything in their life, the good, the bad and the very ugly, we are able to create a beautiful journey that connects directly to the people they are called to serve.

I have always been a lover of stories, an avid reader since a child thanks to my sister, Lisa. We are ten years apart and I wanted to hang out with her at the library. She told me I could only come if I read. I got a library card and feel in love with the fact books can take me places. But something transformational happened when I positioned myself as the storyteller. It is like the situation when you purchase a car and now you see the same car everywhere. I see stories everywhere and as people talk, those words turn into a storyline. I can't turn it off and honestly, I don't want too. Positioning brings placement. It is time to get in position. But all of this cannot happen until you make a decision. You may need to decide differently.

Decisions and anger are powerful catalysts for change. My change in showing up differently came on the heels on a home invasion at gun point. In that moment, I realized how small I was playing. As we waited for law enforcement to arrive, I took a glimpse of my life and knew if this was the end, I had a lot of unanswered questions. What impact did I truly make? What am I currently pursuing? What impact, influence and income am I leaving behind?

Honestly, I'd made no significant impact. Significance doesn't hide, it stands out. That day, I decided I could no longer afford to be the best kept secret. Honestly, being the best but no one knows it doesn't serve anyone well. There must be an intentional decision that you are significant and what you are called to do is significant enough to show up for it. You have a great work to do and people are waiting on you.

V.I.P. QUESTIONS:

Why is what you are called to do significant?

_____

_____

_____

_____

_____

_____

How do you need to position yourself?

_____

_____

_____

_____

_____

_____

What does positioning yourself look like?

_____

_____

_____

_____

_____

_____

V.I.P. (Visibility is Power) Story:

Name: Tamara Brown

Is there a moniker you are known for, i.e. The Rosho Live Storyteller, Live stream strategist and heart felt producer If not, how do you want me to describe you?

Tamara Brown, Not Your Average Trainer, lifestyle & transformation coach.

What does Visibility is Power mean to you?

Visibility is Power, to me means showing up in various places, including media outlets to share your story, adding value to your target market through your content, and positioning yourself as the subject matter expert, so that you are the "Go To" person in your specific industry. Power to me means influence. You only gain influence from people who know, like, & trust you and that only comes from building relationships physically or virtually through various conversations and interactions.

Briefly share your Visibility story.

I thought I was Showing up, until Roshanda Pratt, encouraged me to Go Live on FB, CONSISTENTLY! I had no idea that people were waiting on me to share my story, thoughts, ideas, and strategies to help them on

47

their transformation journey. Since starting a weekly live segment, my social media following (influence) has increased, my clientele has increased, and I've entered into a new realm of sharing my knowledge and being a valuable resource to others who are looking for the solution to their health weight loss problem.

What is your favorite moment since embracing Visibility is Power?

My favorites moments are tied to the feedback and responses from those who are tuning into the weekly segments and the responses from my following who see me showing up differently in my business, on social media, and personal growth.

Advice for those struggling with their visibility?

Do it afraid. Fail forward. It shows your human and relatable

V.I.P. Tip:

Know what problem you are solving, and then show up where your target market is to offer the solutions.

Social media handle:

Facebook.com/notyouraveragetrainer

The Visibility Equation

"You are More Than Enough." -Roshanda E. Pratt

Full disclosure, I was never good at math. Don't tell my kids. I often joke that I am a journalist, and we don't do math. However, in this quest of uncovering and walking in my own visibility I have learned to embrace what I call the visibility equation. The equation goes as follows:

VISIBILITY + CREDIBILITY = PROFITABILITY

If I could break it down, YOU + Your Trustworthiness/Character = Money. Let's start at the beginning with you. There is an economy called you. People buy people. If you are in business, you have heard it said time and time again people want to do business with those they know, like, and trust. One way to build that is by storytelling your Why. Simon Sinek the author of, "Find Your Why" and "Start with Why" offers this truth: "Every one of us has a WHY, a deep-seated purpose, cause or belief that is the source of our passion and inspiration."

Your passion and inspiration are part of YOU and that is an economy. No one else has your experiences, your journey, your story. You matter and no one can beat you at being you. This economy of you is so real that we see it every day in our society. Media mogul, Oprah is a great example. The Oprah effect can take something invisible and catapult it to success. Consider Oprah's favorite things which are truly products she uses and loves. While other celebrities are often paid to promote products, she chooses items which truly capture her interest. She is responsible for using her show to launch the careers of Phillip McGraw a.k.a Dr. Phil, Spiritual guru Iyanla Vanzant and Dr. Oz. One of the most prominent recipients of The Oprah Effect is President Barack Obama.

Her endorsement helped the Illinois senator climb in popularity, arguably helping to lead him to the White House. Still not sure if there is an economy called You? I'm certainly not Oprah, but here is my story of embracing my economy.

1. Early on I owned my visibility and committed to becoming consistent in building an online brand.

2. I created content around my experiences, expertise and know-how.

3. I pushed past the urge to strive for perfectionism and instead embraced progress. Literally, if you committed to becoming 10% better each day by the end of the month you would be 300% better.

4. I carved out a unique spot from my secret sauce. I developed the flavor and took it to market.

The online space can be a brutal reminder of what you are not. We judge our unfiltered lives by someone else's filter. It is cruel punishment to ourselves and creator. There are so many people in the online space and using live video to build their brand it is easy to slip into someone else's persona. When I felt like I was trying to be another person, I took a break from live video and re-adjusted. The problem with showing up as someone else is you attract their audience and not your own. There is a price to not showing up as yourself. It may work for a while. But you are making income off of false pretenses soon people will discover like in The Wizard of Oz, it was all smoke and mirrors. On a deeper level, I masking as someone else is a disservice to God and those you truly are called to impact. There is an audience for you. There is an audience that wants just you. As I told a group of people at a conference once, you are someone's Oprah. Act like it.

When I embraced the essence of me, embraced Roshanda, The Rosho Live, I started framing content around my experiences and used that to teach others. You have experiences and knowledge which can benefit those you are called to impact. I no longer could deny I had to repeat a grade, struggled with my self-esteem, hated my voice and how I looked. But once I healed from those things, I quickly realized the people who I am called to serve. The people who I am called to raise up as messengers struggle with the mess in their message too. The aforementioned is what makes me unique, it is part of my secret sauce. Do YOU know you have a secret sauce?

You have a unique flavor that the people you are called to serve will like. When I began to embrace my own secret sauce, it boosted my confidence and it attracted other people who wanted permission and direction on how to do the same. In my journey, I discovered I spent far too long listening to the enemy's lies. The more I uncovered my message, I realized I am supposed to change the narrative and I want to be in the front because this is where I shine. We must get rid of our stinking thinking when it comes to the gifts within us. God did not make you empty.

Shift from that mindset and remember the 8-year-old girl who wanted to become a teacher, astronaut and president all in a day's work. We have to go back to what gives us no restraints and unimaginable possibilities. I experience and see the unimaginable possibilities every time I use live video. I have met amazing people and business partners, wrote a book about live video that became an Amazon bestseller and I have traveled internationally with my message of visibility. In order to do that, I had to discover my secret sauce and once I did, I had to own it.

Once you own it, then you have to consistently show up as you claim to be. If you are a travel agent that is what I should see and experience. If you are a serial entrepreneur learn how to merge your businesses together or focus on a main thing, grow and expand. Impact usually begins with a person of influence. You are a person of influence. SAY THAT OUT LOUD. I am a person of influence. Let's look at Oprah again.

You and I can both agree she is an influencer. She uses her influence in many different ways. Here are two examples. Oprah makes a book selection pick and the book becomes an instant hit. Oprah talks about beef and shuts down the entire beef industry. Influencers have impact. People listen to influencers; however, being an influencer is not just about popularity. It is about impact.

According to an Inc. Magazine article, an influencer involves five core qualities.

Here are three I want to highlight:

1. *Inspiring others to be more*
2. *Bringing value*
3. *Earning trust and respect*

Bottomline, influencers are people of impact. But you can't impact what you do not show up for. My friend, Kevin, shared with me, there are four reasons people search online: I wanna know; I wanna go; I wanna do; I wanna buy. I believe these four truths can also be applied to live video. We are in an information age and people are hungry for knowledge. If not you, then who? I often say, if you are the one with the answers, then why doesn't anyone know it. Could it be you have not realized who you are? You have not come to terms with your own influence. You don't understand your "why." The people you are called to impact want to be part of a tribe or community. They want a leader to follow. But as my good friend Jennifer Bennett says, "You must be worth following." One way to be worth following is to first realize your worth.

The final part of the visibility equation is Credibility. It is defined as *the quality or power of inspiring belief; capacity for belief.* In the online space, transparency is the new currency, and you have to know how to spend it. I believe credibility is akin to character. People are looking for the real, unfiltered you. My father told me growing up, all you have is your word. My mother drilled in me your name should mean something. While I love social media and the opportunities it has afforded all of us, I also know it has created a culture of phonies. People who are so driven by creating a loose image of truth and selling it for likes.

A *Business Insider* article revealed how people are paying hundreds of dollars to take, 'Rich Kids of Instagram' style photos on a private jet while it sits on the tarmac. Another business article revealed how people are buying clothes to post an outfit of the day only to return it back to the store. We have a culture of keeping up with the Joneses at whatever cost. While people do like these pictures and I am even guilty of stopping and taking a glimpse on Instagram, I am not moved by it.

One of the frequent topics that comes up when it comes to live video, is this notion of perfection. I often tell clients your audience doesn't want perfection, they want progress. Give them the answer they need, be the solution because they are struggling with perfection themselves. The success of Oprah, (I know I use her a lot) rests largely on the fact that she is a real human. She is willing to share her personal story, no matter how tragic and that is why she is so loved. She owned her message and it helped build her credibility.

Why is credibility so important to your visibility? How you show up is how you will be received. Stylist, Soancera Luqmann says, "Dress how you want to be addressed." The same can be said when it comes to how you want people to receive or believe you. Dress or show up how you want to be addressed. I learned especially with live video I cannot show up as anyone else. I do a disservice to God and those I am called to serve. When you show up as someone else, you may attract people, but they will be the wrong people for you.

That is why along with being visible, we also have to be believable. There is so much fake news flooding our timelines, inboxes and television screens. It can be hard to separate fact from fiction. Make it easier for your audience to know you are the real deal. During my final years in television news, I saw how newsrooms would have to fight against the machine of misinformation. We would have people call us on the carpet for not reporting certain information or sharing stories online.

In fact, we created a segment verifying certain news stories and although it was helpful to those blowing up our social media pages, I think it also took away from stories that really needed to be covered because we didn't have the people to do it. Some days in the newsroom, it felt like we were chasing our tails.

In a world of fake news, people are not too eager to trust doing business online. Statistics show 61% of buyers read customer reviews. Why? They want to see what others are saying about you before they commit. I have had people start following my brand: The Rosho Live solely because, "My friend says I need to start watching you." Online is the new word of mouth. Your reputation is valuable, so do not blow it for an opportunity to be seen by certain people. Trust me, it is never worth it. That is what you have to do, build the know, like and trust before you ever ask for their wallet.

How do you build trust? Here is short list although it could be extensive. I will share my short list and give you space to intentionally think about how you are currently building or can build credibility.

5 ways to establish your credibility:

1. **Become the Expert:** In this new era of a digital footprint, it is far easier to validate who you claim to be. Faking it online will only get you so far. Once you establish your authority in how you show up, you begin to build the trust of your audience.

2. **Be the FIRST example:** Whatever you say, whomever you claim to be everything about your online and offline persona should show you walking, the walk. For example, if you are THE best social media strategist, then it should show on your social media pages and website. Basically, live the message you are telling people.

3. **Be consistent in both your business and personal life:** My pet peeve is when I meet people in real life, and they are completely opposite of their social media persona. I get having a bad day or being with your family and wanting personal time. However, the days of separating online and offline personas are no longer. You are one person… one business regardless if you are online or offline. The person I encounter in person should be the same I see online.

4. **Be a source, not a nuisance:** There is a lot of noise in the world. Decide to be a source and not

add to the pollution. What I mean is share information that will make people better. We have enough trash circulating, especially trash that has not been properly vetted. It is so easy to hit the share or like button without doing your due diligence. Explore facts and promote truth both online and in person.

5.   **Build relationships:** Social media has not taken away the art of relationship building. You can find real relationships online, but chances are you are  not taking the time to cultivate them. One of my favorite social media friends, Heather Heuman and I met through a hashtag on Instagram. Take the time to truly build connection with others. Ask questions. Comment on their posts. Reach out to those you are interested in learning more about. For heaven's sake, Be human. It works every time.

Once you merge visibility and credibility together, the outcome is profitability. More trusted visibility equals more potential customers. In business, there is a difference between profit and profitability. Business experts define profit as the amount your business gains. It is a number that remains when you subtract expenses from your revenue.

Profitability measures your business's profits and helps you determine your success or failure. It is not an absolute number. It looks at what your business' profits mean in the form of percentages or decimals. So, what is profitability and not profit? I believe profitability gives an overview and holistic approach to measure how successful you are in the visibility equation. For example, in my home studio, I have a dry erase board with projects broken up by business quarters. It is a trick I learned from Digital Marketer, Ed Troxell. The bible encourages us to write the vision and make it plain. This tactic of writing and assigning tasks to my visibility shows me where I can have impact, influence and income. I can see the opportunities for clear profitability and growth. I can see the places of visibility and credibility in my life and business.

This same visibility equation can be applied to your personal life as well. This is not just for business owners. You can use this equation on your job for your next promotion. You can use this in your family and relationships. Just think about it, we all can be more visible and trustworthy in some way in order to have greater profitability. Here is a practical example from my personal life. I started a healthy regimen of going to the gym in 2017. I started with a trainer and group bootcamp class because I knew for a long time my health and wealth are connected. Here is the equation. I had to get visible for me. I was showing up on stage, live videos, clients, church, and family in pieces. Yes, you heard correctly, in pieces. None of these things really got all of me because I didn't have it to give because of my weight, terrible sleep patterns, and overall unhealthy lifestyle. I had to have a truthful conversation with myself and God.

In my prayer time, I believe God told me how you treat your health, is exactly how you treat your money. He was right. My bank account at the time was overdrawn and so was my body. I had to start building credibility for myself by taking a stand to get my health together. I started having a board meeting with my body at my gym. I started measuring my profitability by my ability to speak on the stage, full of energy and not crash afterwards as well as the downsize in my clothes. Now that's profitable! The result of using this same equation in my personal life with my fitness, has opened the door for a few other people to join me on their fitness journey.

In the book, *Purpose Driven Life* by Rick Warren I think the first line of the book is the most profound. IT IS NOT ABOUT YOU. Even in the visibility equation. I think the greatest profitability I have received has not been monetary, but the profit of collaborations with great businesses and people. Powerful relationships have been created with people who have become extended family members. The people who told me I gave them permission to do the very thing I am encouraging you to do. Someone is waiting on you. You have the solution they need. Your voice matters.

V.I.P. QUESTIONS:

What is your secret sauce?

_____

_____

_____

_____

_____

_____

What does your credibility look like?

_____

_____

_____

_____

_____

_____

How can you build trust or how are you building trust?

_____

_____

_____

_____

_____

_____

V.I.P. (Visibility is Power) Story:

Name: Adrienne Young

Is there a moniker you are known for, i.e., The Rosho Live Storyteller, Live Stream Strategist and Heartfelt Producer If not, how do you want me to describe you?

God's Mouthpiece. Brand and Image Ambassador. Thrifter. Author.

What does Visibility is Power mean to you?

Showing up consistently with content that is valuable to your target market or those who don't even need you (your services) until they encounter you.

Briefly share your Visibility story:

I'd been going live consistently in my private FB group and felt the nudge to teach a Bible study on my nonprofit's public page. Unbeknownst to me, an editor saw the replay, (never underestimate the power of those who watch your replay...be sure to greet them while you're live) of the live and inboxed me this message: "I saw your live. If you ever write a book and need help, let me know." Mind you, I had a book in me and just prayed the day before for God to help me and was very specific in what I needed: editor, self-publishing, how to promote and a book cover. After connecting with the sister in my inbox, she offered everything I prayed for FREE of charge! I landed a book deal because I was visible! Since then, I've written two books with her and formed a business partnership. It has been a ripple effect that I know will last a lifetime.

What is your favorite moment since embracing Visibility is Power?

Running into those who watch me online out in public, hugging, hearing how me going live affected them, and taking selfies!

Advice for those struggling with their visibility?

Just show up. Push the button and go live afraid. You won't regret it as there are people waiting on you and what you have to offer them.

Share your favorite V.I.P. Tip:

Greeting those as they log in and reading their comments from time to time.

Social media handle:

Instagram: @adriennesyoung

The Voice of Visibility

"There is no greater agony than bearing an untold story inside you." -Maya Angelou

Your voice is powerful. I want you to hear yourself say that, so even though this may feel silly, say it out loud… My voice is powerful. But the old adage still rings true, a closed mouth doesn't get fed.

You are broke because no one knows you.

Being seen and being heard starts with being known, known to yourself and known to others. What people experience with me as a marketplace leader, business owner, minister of the gospel all connects to me knowing me first and foremost. I has to become acquitted with myself in all those roles before I introduced myself to the world in those roles. I would say good morning to The Rosho Live. I would practice in the mirror with scriptures as a new minister. In all those instances, I had to give voice to the voice. I had to hear myself in these positions. I didn't just show up as this, I put in some work in becoming visible.

I heard a Jewish Rabbi say, "You can look at your bank account and connect it to the problems you solve." People pay for you to solve their problems. Your invisibility is costing you influence and money. You have expertise, but people don't know it because they don't know you. You deserve to be seen and heard. Don't you think so?

What does it mean to be visible? Noah Webster's 1828 dictionary defines visibility *as the state or quality of being perceivable to the eye; the state of being discoverable or apparent.*

The invention of television media has given influencers, thought leaders, community leaders, servants, brands and businesses, a chance to broadcast to hundreds of thousands in an instant. Social media shrunk that process by giving these same group of people an opportunity to impact with less investment. Jada Pinkett Smith, her daughter and mother created a web television talk show titled *Red Table Talk* on Facebook Watch in 2018. It is widely popular. It is real talk, real topics, with real people. It is important to note the show is produced for Facebook Watch not network. While I still believe the big screen, television, is still vital; social media is nothing to avoid.

In the palm of your hand, you own a network. As a former television news producer, my job was to create a show representative of my community/audience. One way to do that is to have stories people are inspired by, shed light on problems in the community and educate or teach them something my audience may not know. I strongly believed my job as a journalist is to give voice to the voiceless.

There is power in your voice. I think of the women behind the MeToo movement. That movement gained traction and national attention by brave women sharing their stories of sexual harassment and assault. It opened the door for a movement, a social movement through the hashtag: #metoo where women shared openly; some for the first time their stories of sexual harassment or assault. International speaker and coach Cheryl Wood says, "Your story is about you but not for you." Visibility has a voice. All through history we have seen how the power of voice has affected change.

I believe, the power of voice can take on many different forms. Voice can be the printing press, Martin Luther used to publish the gospel. Voice can be a peaceful act of protection like Rosa Parks who refused to give up her seat on a bus to a white man. By using her "voice" she started a boycott and the civil rights movement we still read about today. Voice can be Princess Diana confronting the stigma of HIV during the mid-80's by becoming the first high-profile celebrity to shake hands with an AIDS patient without gloves. At the time, people were fueled by misinformation, that people did not touch sufferers due to the mistaken belief that HIV could be transmitted through contact. Voice is an African American man becoming the first President of the United States. Visibility has a voice that can change the world.

Visibility is Power

Social media gives ordinary people a greater opportunity at being extraordinary. Instead of waiting for a television station to give you a chance, you can create your own media. You can now control the message and your visibility. I know we have heard many times before the start of our movie, silence is golden. But YOUR silence is not golden. That theory may work in the movies but not in real life. Silence is an enemy. Dr. Martin Luther King, Jr. is credited with saying, "Our lives begin to end the day we become silent about things that matter." Think for a moment the stories in our history book. It started with men, women and yes, even children understanding change can't come through silence, but by making some noise. We live in a world full of noise. I am often asked how do you harness the power of your voice in a world full of other voices? Become childlike again. I don't know what happens to us as adults. We become timid, recluse and silent. Most children are not quiet, if they are more than likely there is trouble to follow. Children are audacious. They take risk. In a rather health way, they believe in themselves and their abilities to do it all. Simply put, they are fearless about who they are and who they can become.

When I was in the third grade, I was the child who made fairly decent grades, not much of a troublemaker, but my report always said, "Great student but just talks too much." In a home with West Indian parents, this was like committing the ultimate sin. My parents are traditional. You know, children should be seen and not heard. One day as my father was reading my report card, he saw the grades which were not bad, but honed in on the fact I was talking too much for my teacher's taste. He asked me in a very authoritative voice: What do you have to talk about so?

Now you must understand when Caribbean parents add "so" to the end of a sentence, it is rather serious. I remember it like it happened yesterday, my response. It flowed out of my belly like a river. Without pause or thinking about it, I blurted out very strongly, "I believe I have something to say." My mom looked at me and my father and repeated, "She believes she has something to say." In that moment, I was not sure what would happen. I knew I would get in trouble, but it didn't happen. We all looked at each other for a few moments and then walked away.

Friend, you have to find that little boy or girl who had no problem speaking up. For me, that little girl in third grade who spoke up for herself became lost and silenced in the issues of life. Sexual abuse largely shut my mouth. The predator tells you it is your little secret, no one would believe you or there is no need to say anything about it. Silence comes your norm. I worked past that to find the bold, confident and courageous little girl again. I vowed once I found her, I would not lose her again and I would help others find their voice. When I uncovered my voice and the more I used it on live video, panel discussions and speaking engagements, the more opportunities showed up. For some of you, you are hiding behind logos, lack of money, poor public relations and fear about the mess in your message. Come out, come out, wherever you are.

In 2016, the movie *Hidden Figures* was released about three brilliant African American women at NASA who served as the brains behind one of the greatest operations in US history. The film was set in 1961 when segregation still existed in the United States. While there are still issues of injustice in America, there are far more opportunities now than in previous generations. Innovation and disruption are at our core of advancement. But in order to experience what is available, you have to disrupt thyself. You must understand hiding serves no one. The thought of being the best kept secret is the best kept lie. People follow, people pay, and people listen to those they see. The old adage states, seeing is believing. Make people believe you by seeing you. It is time to step out of the shadows and into the spotlight. How will you shine?

My best work hours are the wee hours of the morning. I attribute that to the overnight shift I worked for many years as a television news journalist. I am talking like 2 am-6am. My husband has never been a fan of my work hours. However, for me it is my best hours for AH-HA moments. This is also the time when I do what I call "inbox" coaching. Any of my clients or close friends can tell you about this. It can be an e-mail, maybe a text, if I know you are awake too, a message through social media.

My sweet friend Jenn was on my radar early one morning when I sent her a message. Jenn is a mom of 6! Yes, 6 kids who are homeschooled. Yes, ladies and gentlemen she is my shero. Jenn has a heart for women and is passionate about Jesus. Every now and again I would see my sweet friend posting on social media words of encouragement and wisdom. It resonated with people.

Early that morning, I sent Jenn a message. In that moment she wasn't my friend, peer or Sister in Christ. We needed to have another conversation as consultant to client. The conversation went like this:

Jenn you have something to say.
The world needs to hear it.
Start writing the devotional.
Now!
You have an audience...
Stop using the kids and other things as an excuse.

That was me using my voice, but I was scared. What if she didn't receive me? What if my friend blocked me from social media and told me to take a hike? Let me be the first to tell you using your voice is risky. Dr. King, Princess Diana and even Jesus Christ all took a risk in using their voice against the status quo. I know my friend was created for more. And especially for mothers, it is easy to sideline your dreams for others. There is a season for everything and if God says this is not the season then obey that, but

I know for many women they use "waiting on God" as an excuse and not as a push to plan while you wait.

So, back to Jenn. This busy wife, mom of 6, homeschool parent, and ministry leader told me she had been praying about taking a leap and the next steps in her purpose. My words, my voice was the catapult she needed. Three months to the date of that "inbox" coaching, I received a message from Jenn. She was featured that weekend on The Today Show parenting blog. They posted her article on their Facebook page and tagged her. She needed me to explain what that meant.

After screaming into the phone, I informed my new client she can now say she was featured on The Today Show parenting blog. WOW! What happened next was amazing and life changing. She was featured again. She also earned a spot to write a series of posts for a national blog. Her Facebook community grew, (Sprinkles in My Closet, Jenn Kish) to 25k organically. Yes, no paid advertisement. Just her authentic and transparent voice. She had a post to go viral, she was written about internationally and created products along with her children to serve her audience. Jenn tapped into showing up and owning her visibility. In just three months, she was able to garner national exposure while still homeschooling, being a wife and mom.

What's your excuse? Who's waiting on you to show up? The best thing you can do is place all the bets on yourself.

Every day you are betting on someone. Why not bet on you? Why not believe in your product or service? Why not trust the value you have to offer? Why not show up authentically in a way which impacts your audience? WHY NOT AND WHY NOT YOU?

According to Dr. King, *"There comes a time when silence is betrayal."* Stop betraying yourself. When you begin to step into your light, use your voice and show up. The people around you start to take notice, they respond. There is something attractive about the person who understands their voice is important to the narrative of the world. Romans 8:19 in the New International Version of the Bible reads, "*For the creation waits in eager expectation for the children of God to be revealed.*" Every time I think about quitting-shrinking back, I think about the women who would be impacted. When I wrote my first book, *CEO Of Live Video*, I was nearing delivery of our baby girl. Not really an ideal time to write a book. I was challenged, really dared to do it. The little girl in me who doesn't like to be told she can't, did it.

While having Braxton Hicks, uncomfortable and stressed, I wrote that book. Through tears, I pushed ahead despite feeling the weight literally was too much to bare. Have you ever been there? While speaking at a social media summit, I realized why there seemed to be so much opposition in releasing this book. I have learned challenges aren't necessarily a warning that I am to stop, but rather a clarion call I am right where I am supposed to be. When opposition attempts to knock on your door, don't you dare quit. The very presence of challenges are proof that you are heading in the right direction.

At that event in Nashville, a woman purchased my book. I took the time to speak with her as I felt led to do so. I prayed with her, not unusual for me. The next day, I discovered she was one of the sponsors of the event. She took to the stage and shared her story. She revealed she had not planned to do so but felt compelled once reading my book. Then she said directly to me in front of everyone, she did not plan on going live, but my book convicted her to live! She revealed she had been struggling with depression. She discovered, from a book I wrote about using live stream, the power of her voice and her life. In that moment, I realized what I am doing is so much bigger than teaching how to push a button to Go Live. But my mission is to raise up messengers, thought leaders, and influencers.

These are people persuaded to shape the culture and change the narrative. You and I can't afford to quit. One of my favorite quotes is by Mark Twain. He is credited with saying: "The two most important days in your life are the day you are born and the day you find out why." When we start to step into our light, whether it's a limelight of visible success or the light of living from a place of more contentment/joy/love/power, the people around us will have a response.

I was speaking to a group of millennial professionals about living your life as if you are negotiating for someone else. It is often easier to tell someone else what to do than taking your own advice. The same is true for being seen and heard. If you live your life, not *for* others, but to *impact* others, it makes all the difference in the world.

So, how are you using the power of your voice? I want you to really consider that question up until this point how have you valued your own voice? You have valued the voice of others and Yes, that is important. But the person who you believe and follow the most, is yourself. You believe you, before you believe me. How you respond to the sound of your voice is essential. I did a training on how singers have to push through their own physical and emotional challenges that can cause strain on their voices. Much like singers, life can cause us physical and emotional challenges which causes strain on our voices too.

In an article in *Psychology Today*, experts mentioned a few things singers bring into practice that cause them not to show up fully.

1.   What they say to themselves consciously or un-consciously.
2.   Fear of failure.

3.   Fear of success.
4.   Fear of being known.
5.   Personal insecurities.

Can you see yourself in one or more of the above? The number 1 way experts encourage singers to push pass this is by knowing and owning their worth.

Researchers say when singers embrace their worth and get confident in their voice, their performance changes for the good. Like singers, we have improved technique, confidence, pitch and stage presence. Your voice is an instrument. You embrace your voice and have a greater presence. The bottom line: when you push back what's trying to muzzle you and embrace your instrument you operate in your zone of genius with confidence and ease. No one can take that from you. Your voice is a blessing from God. "The blessing of the Lord brings wealth, without painful toil for it." Proverbs 10:22 NIV. Allow your voice to be His mouthpiece. Respect your voice and don't betray it and understand part of your showing up is also part of your speaking up in a way that impacts, heals and gives others permission to come out of the shadows. You need to be seen and heard.

I strongly believe speaking differently leads to seeing differently. Your vision is connected to your voice. You see what you say. Vision in visibility is so vitally important.

Much of what we discussed connects to how we see ourselves. It is true visibility is power but without a vision there is no power. There are several definitions for sight according to the 1828 Noah Webster dictionary. Vision is actual sight; the faculty of seeing and revelation from God. How are you seeing things, really?

Imagine with me you are traveling in your car on a rainy day. For many of us, turning on your windshield wipers in order to see makes sense, right? The whole point is to minimize the impact of the rain to prevent your vision being impeded while driving. But many of us go through life with limited vision which causes us to see things through a filtered perspective. I think we can agree when I turn on the windshield wipers during the rain my ability to see is much better.

Your words have a similar effect on your life. Your vision for your life will only manifest as high as you speak. God has bigger, do you see it? If you do see it, you must speak it. Say what you see, to receive what you say. This is so powerful for me because much of what I am walking in happened in the invisible before it ever manifested itself in the natural. To truly be seen you must have a greater perspective of the importance of your voice and a vision for that voice. Voices help shift cultures and God is still looking for culture shapers. Become convinced your voice matters. Make a decision to see differently in order to speak differently so you can receive what you say.

77

V.I.P. Questions

How can you embrace your voice?

_____
_____
_____
_____
_____
_____

What has prevented you from releasing your voice?

_____
_____
_____
_____
_____
_____

What is one way you can use your voice to come out of the shadows?

_____
_____
_____
_____
_____
_____

What is your God inspired vision? Be as detailed as possible

_____

_____

_____

_____

_____

_____

_____

_____

_____

_____

_____

_____

_____

_____

_____

_____

_____

_____

_____

_____

_____

_____

_____

_____

_____

_____

_____

_____

V.I.P. (Visibility is Power) Story:

Name: Jennifer Kish

Is there a moniker you are known for? i.e. The Rosho Live Storyteller, Live Stream Strategist, and Heartfelt Producer. If not, how do you want me to describe you?

Writer and Speaker at Sprinkles in My Closet Blog

What does Visibility is Power mean to you?

Visibility is power means that if I am brave enough to show up and speak up, then I will be able to influence those around me.

Briefly share your Visibility story:

In March of 2018, Roshanda encouraged me to "show up." In her challenge, she recommended that I write a blog post every single day and submit my writing to outlets to be published. I followed her instructions and within three months, I was published on two national sites. One of those sites was NBC's The Today Show. On the day that Roshanda challenged me, my Facebook following was hovering around 300; today I have over 26,000 followers. Visibility is Power converted my hobby into a business.

What is your favorite moment since embracing Visibility is Power?

My favorite moment has to be the opportunity to speak at a church in NC on Palm Sunday. It was my first opportunity to speak at a Sunday morning service.

Advice for those struggling with their visibility?

You have to do the work. You can't wonder what everyone will think. Be confident in your calling and take the first step.

V.I.P. Tip (share your favorite Visibility tip i.e using Live Video to connect to your audience)

Roshanda gave great advice about how to dress for live interview that has stuck with me. She advised that we treat it like a job interview and that has challenged me to be at my best when I press that Live button.

Social media handle:

FB: @SprinklesInMyCloset

The Responsibility of Visibility
"Those who tell the stories rule the world."
-Native American Proverbs

I t would be irresponsible if I did not tell you while finding your voice, building credibility and your visibility is a life changing journey, there is also a profound level of responsibility operating at this level. You just read the story of Jennifer Kish. The mom of 6 who built her visibility, organic following of over 25k and business in about 14 months. She put in some work. The same can happen for you. But with that came something Jennifer had to contend with. She had her first negative comment. I could tell it stung. I remember my first negative comment after becoming a social media correspondent for a day on CBS' The Talk. The comment stung. I told myself if only they knew me. As if, I wanted to be friends with this person. Since then, I have made a personal rule, never read the comments on public posts outside of my own community. The old adage says, sticks and stones may break my bones, but words will never hurt me is a BIG FAT LIE! Words are powerful and they can hit like a sledgehammer. In this moment of dealing with my first negative comment, I had to remember this person does not know me. Although they matter to God, they did not matter to where I was headed. I know easier said than done, right?

I offered a few words to Jennifer when she reached out to me. Things like it is not always a good idea to read comments especially on a big platform where opinions are like belly buttons, everyone has one and few know what to do with it. You can also set filters on your page to hide certain comments. In addition to those things, I also told her hold on to the words that do matter.

My two decades working in a newsroom and answering the phone with complaints from viewers like she is too fat, I hate her eyebrows, her make-up is terrible, her voice drives me crazy and that lipstick makes her look like a slut. I have seen my share of reporters/anchors crying at their desk because people feel they can call and say anything from the other side of a phone. Social media did not help quench that desire to tear down others either. We have keyboard cowards who are brazen enough to say these things on social media. I applaud those who tactfully call these people out. When you shine, there is always someone who is going to try to dull your shine. Always. Your response is to continue to shine. I have learned someone else's insecurities about themselves should not affect me. There are people who will not be able to handle your new-found freedom, but you cannot take that on as your issue. The more you embrace your visibility, you can start questioning yourself, doubting and even worrying about the person who may be trying to shut you down. Here are a few things to consider:

1. People who shut down, criticize or rarely celebrate are probably suffering. It can be heard to deal with feelings of your own inadequacy, to see others shining and aware of what's missing in your life or how you still hiding in the shadows. Remember what I said, stories give permission. Your story can reveal what they are not operating in. It is NOT your job to pull or drag them into being seen. It is not your job to flaunt it either. Pray for them, be an encouragement but do not shrink back in hopes that will help them. Playing small does not help anyone.

2. The person could be dealing with a scarcity mentality. They believe your shine is all there is and there is none for them.

3. People who shut down, criticize and rarely celebrate betray the gift of God on the inside of them. This does not bring them any closer to step into their own visibility.

As you can see, the lack of support has nothing to do with you. Do not take it personal. Decide to be responsible for your actions and responses, nothing more. One day I was moaning and groaning about who was not supporting me and what I needed from, "them." I was politely reminded instead of focusing on what is not supporting, who is not here, how about focusing on who is here and being supportive. We spend far too much time focused on what is not which often prevents us from focusing on what is.

There is still much more you have to work on in this new role of being visible. Along with dealing with people who may have a problem with your freedom to be seen and heard, you also have to contend with the little girl or boy within. I encourage you to find the boldest or confidence of that little person within, but we must be careful the little person within, doesn't stop us from growing up. At some point, the mature you will have to take a front seat and leave behind childish things.

The places I have been and continue to go I can't take the third grade girl with me. Although, she boldly spoke up then, I needed the mature girl now. For many clients I work with, one of the hurdles they must clear is still identifying with the "little" boy or girl in your life. When I started to embrace my visibility, starting the journey of finding my voice, I had to become the spokesperson of my own life before I could do it for others. I had to mature pass the 8-year-old girl who declared she had something to say to truly walk out that idea.

I realized I had two competing voices in my head and had to silence one in order to go to the next. The third grade,

Roshanda served me well in finding my voice again but the stages, boardrooms and media I was entering in, I needed the mature woman there. In simple terms, I needed the boldness of the third grader but the maturity and growth of the woman that is now Roshanda. Isaiah 6:5-8 reads,

"Woe to me!" I cried. "I am ruined! For I am a man of unclean lips, and I live among a people of unclean lips, and my eyes have seen the King, the Lord Almighty." Then one of the seraphim flew to me with a live coal in his hand, which he had taken with tongs from the altar. With it he touched my mouth and said, "See, this has touched your lips; your guilt is taken away and your sin atoned for." Then I heard the voice of the Lord saying, "Whom shall I send? And who will go for us?" And I said, "Here am I. Send me!"

Understand this, before recognizing he was ready and able to go, there is a whole exchange of preparation in verses 5-6. A time of repentance, healing and anointing. Part of the responsibility of being visible is understanding the work you must do in embracing the mess in your message. I tell clients all the time you must make sure you are healed from your past so that you do not bleed over people. We have enough people doing that.

Visibility is Power

When I traveled to Paris, France for my first international speaking engagement I shared what I called my Swan Song. The Tedx style talk dealt with my very transparent journey from ugly duckling to swan. The idea is based on this ancient idea Swans are quiet until death when they sing their final song. The idea is all of us have to die to something in order to release our voices. What are you willing to die to in order to be visibly responsible?

A client we will call Samantha, reached out to me with a dilemma. She noticed the more she showed up, the more people would inbox her with requests asking for her to be their mentor, if they could take her out for coffee or discussion about partnership. For someone who wasn't getting that visibility, who wasn't getting that response previously, it became overwhelming. Imagine, you go from invisible to visible, the new "IT" girl in a matter of what seems like moments. This is what happens when you start owning your space and really showing up like a giant. You attract people who want the light. They want to be in your space, they want to do business with you. Samantha told me while she likes it, and she is making more money, she doesn't know what to do now.

Maybe you're experiencing the same thing, or you can see that in your future. I told her you set the perimeters. You don't have to go out to lunch with everyone who asks. You are not required to mentor people if God doesn't want you to serve in that way. You get to decide what that responsibility looks like.

For example, I felt a real urge to mentor millennial women. After several inbox messages from various professional and entrepreneurial millennials asking for time with me, I knew I had to reach the group and not one on one. I committed to a night of mentorship once a quarter. The women showed up and were appreciative of my time. Your audience will demand more, but you decide what more looks like. What can you do to be responsible with the light you have been given? Never leave that in the hands of someone else to decide. I advised my client Samantha to weigh every conversation she has with people who claim to want her.

Here goes the word intention again. I don't think we are intentional enough about relationships we want to create and grow. One thing I noticed while in Paris, the Parisian people are very intentional about food and the company they keep. Mealtime in America seems like a chore, but in Paris it is an experience, sitting hours talking or not, chewing their food and enjoying the experience. AHHH, take me back now!

My family and I visited the Smithsonian's National Museum of African American History and Culture in Washington, D.C. What an eye-opening experience. I have studied African- American history, but this was a walk in my ancestors' shoes. I walked away with a greater sense of the power of visibility. While a culture tried to keep many men, women and children hidden and invisible, they still decided, even at the risk of their own lives, to show up and challenge the status quo. They knew the responsibility of not doing so.

Our stories give others permission. Whatever that story may be, whether it is you showing up or not you are still telling a story. I always knew growing a platform goes beyond performance. It is when preparation and opportunity meet, and you decide to show up. My encounter with this truth happened at a social media conference. A woman purchased my book. No big deal, right? But what happened the next day at the conference has left a lasting impression. I found out the next day she was a major financial backer of the conference. From the stage she shared how at 4 in the morning she was reading my book. She told a room full of people she was not going to do a live video, but my book convicted her to go live. Whoa! I was speechless. She then went on to say everyone at the conference needed my book and she purchased all the books I had, more than two dozen!

What she did not know is how much pain, struggle and life work I went through with my first self-published book: *CEO Of Live Video*. My book is about supporting people to be seen in live video, but this woman discovered being seen in life. Her public endorsement of the book not only transformed her life, but it also transformed the lives of everyone in attendance who purchased the book because of her on-stage support. To take it a step further, the lives of everyone who watched the live videos of those who purchased the book were also transformed! All these people were impacted because one woman stood in and embraced the responsibility of her visibility.

When you realize that for many people your message is life and death literally you take your showing up seriously. What I have discovered is that while I may not be everyone's cup of tea, to someone else I am life-saving water and I am okay with that. You must realize as you come into who you are there will be some who do not understand. But that is the 'occupational hazard' that comes with showing up. You put yourself in a position to be criticized, judged and even mocked. But the beauty I choose to focus on is the fruit which comes from me being responsible with my visibility. I choose to focus on the many encounters I have had like the one with Mary. I focus on the parents who tell me their children watch my videos online, the proud look in my children's eye, the high-five from my husband, and the support from too many others to name.

The bottom line: World changers will always get push back especially when you are confronting systems that need to change. This is part of being a V.I.P. Embrace the responsibility of showing up, factor it in, and move forward anyway. The definition of responsibility is the state of being accountable or answerable, as for a trust or office, or for a debt. My Pastor says: Our debt to society is payable through people. Visibility is a service. This is not about popularity. This is about making God known to people. Although you will make impact, gain influence, and profit from your visibility, there is a greater purpose attached to your life and visibility. You are ultimately responsible for the following: How you show up, what you say when you show up, and the results from what you did when you showed up. This is why everything we do as V.I.P.ers (YES, I am making this a thing) is vitally important.

Think about everyone in history. We read and discuss those people who understood the responsibility over their life. We all have a duty, a purpose, a call to be here. It grinds my gears when I see people misusing or mishandling their visibility. Just because you 'can', whatever the can is, doesn't mean you should. Visibility is Power is what you stand in but what you do with it is about others. Respond to your responsibility. Trust me there is more working for you than what could be working against you.

V.I.P. QUESTIONS

Where have you been irresponsible concerning your
visibility? List specific areas

_____

_____

_____

_____

_____

_____

How can you become more responsible with your
visibility?

_____

_____

_____

_____

_____

_____

What is one way you can use your voice to come out
of the shadows?

_____

_____

_____

_____

_____

_____

V.I.P. (Visibility is Power) Story:

Name: Andrea Harrison

Is there a moniker you are known for? ie. The Rosho Live Storyteller, Live stream strategist and heart felt producer. If not, how do you want me to describe you?
Founder of Unleash Your Brilliance

What does Visibility is Power mean to you?

Visibility is Power is a powerful attraction marketing strategy that gives your clients and customers the opportunity to get to know, like and trust you. For people who don't know you or know that you exist, in my opinion, it's a guaranteed way for them to find you and connect with you. The more visible you are, the greater your impact on the world you were created to serve!

Briefly share your Visibility story:
One of my greatest life struggles has been my weight. Over the past two years, it's really bothered me the most, probably because I am now in the "spotlight", so to speak. As a leader and a speaker, I am now in a position of "influence" and many people look up to me. However, I understand that God is using my platform to carry out my purpose through what I am most passionate about, inspiring women! With that being said, I allowed my weight and

94

how I felt about the way I looked to put a pause on unleashing my brilliance. When you listen to the grumblings of the enemy, you start to believe that you are not worthy, you are not valuable, you are not beautiful and that you have no purpose.

There have been two specific periods of time during the last two years where I allowed those thoughts to stop me from walking in my purpose. Choosing to listen to the lies of the enemy rather than believe the promises of God! I remember being asked to speak at a conference in front of about 300 people and my first thoughts were, "why me?" Feeling inadequate and wondering why anyone would want to listen to anything I had to say; the lies started to take root in my mind.

I almost cancelled. I kept thinking that I wasn't enough. In fact, those were the exact words running through my mind. I never shared those thoughts with anyone. About 5 days before I was scheduled to speak, a lady from the homeschool community we were a part of at the time, sent me a message on Facebook. She is a very sweet lady. We didn't really know each other. We communicated through Facebook about homeschool, table décor, jewelry and other light topics. We saw each other a hand full of times at homeschool events, but we never shared anything too deep. The day after my birthday, days away from this speaking engagement, she sent me a message on Facebook that rocked my world!

She wrote, "I know it's late, but I cannot wait any longer. I feel this in my spirit for you. I hear God saying, "who told you you're not good enough? Who told you, you won't succeed?" Satan is the father of all lies and in him, there is no truth. God has called you to this and He will see you through it. God says, "remember the vision I gave you for the journey? I have called you. Who took the wind out of your sails?" She went on to say, "put the devil under your feet, woman of God and rise up! I am leading you, don't try to do this in the flesh, but by my spirit says the Lord!" By this time, I can barely see through the tears. She ends with, "You are appreciated, wanted, needed and life fills the room when you walk into it. He hears you and He sees you, my friend. Take it to Him and continue to fight the good fight. Don't let the enemy lie to you anymore filling your head with nonsense!"

OH MY GOODNESS!!! Like seriously? Did this lady just lay me out? How did she know? These were my exact thoughts that she spoke to me and we've NEVER as much as had a conversation! I knew then that this was truly the heart of God being shared with me and I decide to RISE UP! I cannot even begin to tell you how many good things came out of me speaking at that event! Not just for me, but for many other people. That speaking engagement led to another one and another one and the testimonies just kept coming about how God used to me to impact many lives! One sweet lady said through her own tears, "it was because of you that I didn't go through with ending my life." I thought to myself, what if I did cancel? All of these women would never have received their breakthrough or their blessing. If I didn't show up and use my voice to share my story, what would happen to the hundreds of women whose lives were touched? If I continued to believe the lies that I wasn't enough, had nothing to say and was too fat to be considered impactful, what would happen to the women whose destinies were attached to my purpose?

What is your favorite moment since embracing Visibility is Power?

My favorite moment since embracing Visibility is Power, is watching others embrace it as well. It's so refreshing to see women, who all their lives have been told they weren't enough, throw off the cloak of guilt and shame and stand in their genius.

Advice for those struggling with their visibility?

NIKE said it best, "Just Do it". It's as simple as that! Don't get caught up in 'selfish thoughts'. We often say, "We GO LIVE so others CAN LIVE". You can't worry about what you look or sound like when there are literally people dying because you refuse to OPEN YOUR MOUTH and USE YOUR VOICE to TELL YOUR STORY! There are people whose destiny is attached to your purpose, if you refuse to show up, they never will. Yeah! It's that deep!

V.I.P. Tip:

GO LIVE!!! If you are nervous about it, perhaps try interviewing someone else, therefore the spotlight will not be on you, however, you will still be visible.

Website:

www.unleashyourbrilliancetoday.com

Visibility is Power

The VIP Challenge

"Do not go where the path may lead, go instead where there is no path and leave a trail." -Ralph Waldo Emerson

Why are you so passionate about this Roshanda? I probably should have stated this at the beginning of the book, but it happened in 2013, in what I like to call my burning bush experience. As I mentioned in Chapter 4, in 2013, I realized just how important impact is. My family and I were victims of a home invasion at gunpoint. My husband encountered the gunman in the hallway and ran back in our bedroom to protect me. My husband is cool as a cucumber. I will never forget his cool but concerned voice. As he pulled me out of the bed and onto the floor as it was early in the morning, I was so confused by what was happening. When I heard the man push in our door and ask for our money and jewelry, I immediately remembered my time in the news station covering home invasions. My prayer: Please God, do not let this be more than one person. Please God, do not let him kill us.

You never realize how fragile and how quick life can end when you are staring down a gun pointed at you and your loved ones. After the masked gunman left, I became acutely aware of my significance. My thought is this, if the enemy could be that brazen to come on my property and threaten my life, it must be valuable. A thief does not come for what does not have value.

Until that point, I was not serious enough about my calling, how I impact the world nor how I show up. I treated my business, my calling, like a hobby and it produced like one. That home invasion served as a major wake-up call: GIRL, TIME TO SHOW UP FOR REAL! That day I asked myself what would be said of me if this truly was the end? That home invasion saved my life. That day I vowed to start the journey becoming a mouthpiece and using my voice as an instrument. I started taking real steps in making my visibility a non-negotiable, impactful and profitable. But to do any of those things I had to confront the woman in the mirror. I had to start seeing myself, expertise and everything surrounding my visibility differently. There was a lot of mindset shifting, challenging my self-talk and my thinking around who I really am and how to show up in that fully.

It has been a journey to get to a place where I can see the power of standing in who God created me to be. I hope you see that for yourself too. Visibility is Power is beyond a mantra on a shirt. It is my life mission to equip women, a few brave men and children to understand being seen and heard is in God's plan for His creation.

One definition for the word image is show. In the creation story found in Genesis 1:26-28 God said, "Let us make man in Our image..." Let me translate that. Let us make man in our show. We are supposed to be on display, showing God's glory in the earth. My favorite Native American Proverb says, those that tell the stories rule the world. Maybe the world you are called to rule is a bit darker because you have not put God's glory on display. The problem is we live in a world that shows a lot of flash and less substance. A world based on falsehoods and lies.

100

When we become clear on our visibility, accept our voice and the responsibility that comes with it, this is an act of showing God in life, business and ministry. Visibility is power is an assignment.

You can no longer ignore your assignment. Visibility is your responsibility when you partner with you to provide the opportunities. If you have not realized by now true visibility is an inside job. While the world will tell you to focus on the outside. Do the work; create the business, the message, the email campaign, etc, etc, etc. There is nothing wrong with those things, but we often spend so much time doing and not being. Visibility is an inside job. My challenge to you is to start the journey of the inside work. God created you in His image and likeness. He created you from himself. What you are born to create, and impact starts on the inside and it will manifest on the outside. A wise man or woman draws out what's on the inside but that which is on the inside is what refreshes others. Cheryl Wood who wrote our beautiful foreword is credited with saying; playtime is over. I agree. It's time to show up. Your visibility is **V**ital, **I**mpactful and **P**rofitable. **You are a V.I.P.**

V.I.P. Questions

What are you passionate about?

_____
_____
_____
_____
_____
_____

How have you added work to what you passionate about?

_____
_____
_____
_____
_____
_____

How are you refreshing others?

_____
_____
_____
_____
_____
_____

VISIBILITY IS POWER CONFESSIONS:

I believe in the power of we have what we say. The person you believe most is yourself. This is a short list of the confessions I make. My prayer you will find these helpful on your journey of visibility.

> When I open my mouth, God will fill it with good things (Psalm 81:10)
> I give myself permission to be seen and heard (Matthew 5:14)
> I will use the power of my voice to bring good news with peace, love and good tidings (Romans 10:8, Isaiah 52:7)
> My voice matters (Psalm 45:1)
> I am the solution (Romans 8:19)
> I am not afraid of my voice and standing in my own visibility because God stands with me (Isaiah 41:10)

V.I.P. (Visibility is Power) Story:

Name: Fraendy Clervaud

Is there a moniker you are known for, i.e., The Rosho Live Storyteller, Live Stream Strategist and Heart felt Producer If not, how do you want me to describe you?
TrendyFraendy

What does Visibility is Power mean to you?
As an entrepreneur, you must position yourself so that your brand/services get the public traction that it needs. However, at the same time, you must be prepared and intact so your visible brand/service makes a lasting impact!

Briefly share your Visibility story:
"Faith.Family.Fashion" are all three facets that make up TrendyFraendy. I wanted my brand to not only represent me, but people who are open about their faith in Christ Jesus, those who love their family/life enrichment and those who appreciate modest fashion.

What is your favorite moment since embracing Visibility is Power?
Having the opportunity to own my image, brand and what best represents me.

Advice for those struggling with their visibility?

Honestly, there is a season for everyone. Growing up, my parents often told me this Haitian-Creole proverb, "Pari pat bati yon sel jow." Meaning, it will take time before you can cultivate all that you need to be successful. In a world of social media, I encourage others to work on their craft and be patient. You don't have to rush to prove yourself to anyone. This reminds me of the scripture that says, "A man's gift makes room for him and brings him before great men."

Share your favorite V.I.P. Tip:
As you connect with your viewers, image and background is very important. If you are indoors, make sure you have a background that looks professional. When a viewer sees that your live background and video quality are professional, they are more prone to listen to what you have to say and regard you as credible. Also make sure you address your viewers as you go along.

Social media handle:
IG: @trendyfraendy

Visibility is Power

Bonus Chapter: The Hope of Visibility
Written by Jacobee Pratt

"Hold fast to dreams, for if dreams die life is a broken-winged bird, that cannot fly" -Langston Hughes

There was a sailor who was out at sea. This was something he did periodically as a hobby. He would take his sailboat out on the sea, sail for hours, then return to the dock and go home. This particular day, he wanted to be more adventurous and went out a little farther than he normally would. While out, he encountered some rough seas and was knocked around, causing him to be disoriented. He was able to outlast the roughness of the sea, however he no longer knew where he was or which direction he needed to sail to get to land. He chose a course and began sailing again, not really knowing whether he was going in the right direction. As he was sailing in his chosen direction, it began getting dark and now he was not able to really see where he was going. He sailed and sailed. He was on the sea for hours, not having a means to contact anyone. He had thoughts of whether he would ever reach land or would he be lost at sea forever. As he was imagining the worst and about to lose hope, in the distance he saw a lighthouse! All the anxiety, worry, and fear went away. The thought of despair dissipated. It was not because he saw land or because he saw people. It was because he saw the lighthouse.

You may be asking yourself, what was the point of that story? Well, I have discovered that words and pictures dominate the soul. I needed you to get a picture of someone lost at sea and imagine their anxiety and despair. I needed you to be able to imagine you being the one lost at sea. Many times, we do not understand the gravity of a situation until we put ourselves in it.

In the previous chapters of this book, my wife has been uncovering for you the importance of your "visibility" as well as how you need to be "seen, heard, and paid!" She has expressed to you that your visibility is power, impact, and it is profit. What a profound concept! The impact and profitability you have been waiting on has been hiding inside your visibility this whole time. My assignment in this chapter is not rehearse those concepts, but to give a new insight into this mandate called "Visibility."

There is hope in your visibility. In the above story, the man was beginning to lose hope in whether he would ever be able to get back to land. Then something happens for him that changed everything. A lighthouse became visible to him. Imagine that! A building that just had a spinning light in it, gave him hope.

This is what I want you to remember; what may be insignificant to you, is significant to someone else. You are the lighthouse and there are people who are lost at the sea of life that need you to be visible. Your visibility will bring you profit and yes, you should be paid, however, getting paid cannot be your sole motive for wanting to be visible. You should want to provide light and hope to those who are lost in the "mess" of their life. As you have read previously, there is a "mess" in your "message" and people need to hear and see how you navigated out of your mess. Your "mess-age" gives them hope.

Let us look deeper into the purpose of a lighthouse. Lighthouses have a two-fold purpose; to be a navigational aid and to warn boats of dangerous areas. Lighthouses are usually located on rocky cliffs, near dangerous reefs, or a harbor. There are people you have influence with who are trying to navigate through their lives and are headed towards dangerous reefs and cliffs. If you do not give light to them, they will most likely become shipwreck. I'm sure you can think of a few people right now who fit that description.

There are others who may not be on the verge of being shipwreck but have been at sea for many days. These people have lost their direction, do not know where to turn and are on the verge of losing hope. This is where your lighthouse (sorry, your visibility) is needed. Just as the lighthouse tells a sailor who has been on the water for a long time and is looking for land, "Come this way." Your story, your visibility should be calling to others saying, "Come this way." Come this way in media; Come this way in business; come this way in parenting; come this way in whatever area of their lives they need to find the shore. Do not allow your mess ups, mistakes, and past failures put out the light that will light the way for others.

Do you remember what it was like when you were trying to find your way? Do you still remember how you felt when you were in that dark place of your life? Who was it that gave you light? Whose life shined and gave light to you so that you could find your way out of the darkness? It is your turn to be that for somebody else.

Your visibility is power, impact, and profit. As of the date that you are reading this, your visibility is hope! It is hope for the mom that wonders if she can be about her business and still raise great children. It is hope for the person who has a horrific past and questions whether or not their life still matters. It is hope for the couple who wants to have a great marriage but has had difficulty loving one another. There are lives who need to see you. There are lives searching for the light that your story brings. Hit the "go live" button on your life and begin to give the light of hope to those who need it. In other words, let's be visible!